SWEET SURVIVAL

poems by

Pamela Smith

Finishing Line Press
Georgetown, Kentucky

SWEET SURVIVAL

Copyright © 2017 by Pamela Smith
ISBN 978-1-63534-325-0 First Edition
All rights reserved under International and Pan-American Copyright Conventions. No part of this book may be reproduced in any manner whatsoever without written permission from the publisher, except in the case of brief quotations embodied in critical articles and reviews.

ACKNOWLEDGMENTS

"Routine" appeared as "IDDM" in T*he Art of Medicine in Metaphors: A Collection of Poems and Narratives,* ed. James Borton with Brandi Ballard
"After" appeared without title in *Just These Three Lines* co-authored with Bee Smith
"Diabetes Makes a Confession" and "Diabetes Applauds Itself" were composed for a trialogue presented at the conclusion of "Poetry, Prose, and Prayer," a Lilly-funded workshop with Dennis Michael Browne at the Institute for Ecumenical and Cultural Research, St. John's University, Collegeville, MN, 2015.
"Prescription" is adapted from a portion of "Sweet Survival" (a prose piece), which appeared in *The Art of Medicine in Metaphors*
"The Pier at Folly Beach" appeared in *Surrounded: Living with Islands,* ed. Sheryl Clough

Publisher: Leah Maines

Editor: Christen Kincaid

Cover Photo: Pamela Smith

Author Photo: Deirdre Mays, Roman Catholic Diocese of Charleston

Cover Design: Elizabeth Maines McCleavy

Printed in the USA on acid-free paper.
Order online: www.finishinglinepress.com
        also available on amazon.com

Author inquiries and mail orders:
Finishing Line Press
P. O. Box 1626
Georgetown, Kentucky 40324
U. S. A.

Table of Contents

Body Slam 1
Shot at 22 2
Compliance 4
Simpaticos 5
Routine 6
After 8
Another 3 A.M. 9
Making Tracks 12
PTSD 13
Diabetes Makes a Confession 14
Number 15
One Blue Heron 16
Three Cars 17
Forgetting Pain 20
Prescription 21
The Pier at Folly Beach 22
The Stories 23
To David Sedaris 24
More Than a Curriculum Vitae 25
Diabetes Applauds Itself 26
Getting Started 27
Adventure 28

Body Slam

It's awfully hard to focus on matters of spirituality and poesy when you've just taken a body slam. The one which has generated the subject matter and style of this collection was the diagnosis which sent me to Delaware Valley Hospital and has needled me ever since.

Yet somehow life with an aggravating chronic illness has prompted meditative moments and books. In 2019 it will be 50 years—not of slam, but sweet survival.

Shot at 22

Part 1

Back then they bedded you down for eight days,
an unsung octave of rest and tests.
They explained why they were
dipsy-doodling and puncturing you,
sampling anything that streamed
into fine vials and cups.

That first night the injection fizzed into you
and hit a few hours later like slo-mo scattershot.
You dropped into unmuscled panic,
loose as Oz's scarecrow,
and rang bells only for them to tell:
Oh, by the way, this is called insulin shock.

They shot you A.M. and P.M.,
then bypassed the oft-told oranges
when it was time for your first try.
You hit your own rind, pinching
your recently thinned-down thigh.

You tinkled copiously,
and, since you were a tad anemic,
they ironed you deluxe
until your stool turned black.
They taught you how to drop tablets
into dribbles of your own urine.

This became life support or some such,
poured into a dainty test tube
housed in its own home-sweet-home kit.
You learned to color-compare, check boxes,
and, oh yeah, bring the little log to the doc
on what would become your frequent visits.

They had you read about the poppy fields—
not Dorothy's or the Tin Man's or Toto's
but the tiny exudates that might proliferate
across the backfields of your eyes.
And told you, sorry, after 20 years or so
you might go blind.

Wild monkeys tussled and screeched and teased.
They mussed your sleep.

Part 2

And so you lived,
all your sick days that year poofed away
like a sneak attack of cyclone
or overdose of witchery.
But you worked.
And you measured what you ate.

Next to no one among your Age of Aquarius soulmates
thought fruit juice and austerity
counted as going out for a drink.
You'd apparently lost them: the ruby shoes
to click through opiate fields or dance down yellow brick roads
en route to the Emerald City.

Compliance

Well,
now that you mention it,
yes.

The orbit
is not a perfect circle
but, rather,
an ellipse.

Simpaticos

Sometimes it's the snack-equipped kid in school or the grouchy one in the camp for diabetic children who reminds you that there are people much younger than you who are medical kin. You know you need to hug them.

Sometimes it's the rescue Sheltie who by mere smell rather than training becomes your weather radio, sending out alerts at every hint of blood drop. You know that when the time comes to put her down you will hold her and hum a lullaby as she slumps into her final sleep.

Routine

The diabetic 8-year-old informs his teacher,
"If they poke any more holes in me,
they can use me for a lawn sprinkler."
Michelle, 13, tells how she's sick of it.
She has no metaphors like his.

Gail and Tony, both 17, stage a fling,
declare a diabetes-free day. They drop injections,
carouse arm in arm to ice cream shops,
slug down sweet Cokes,
lunch like funnels on fries with mega-burgers,
and chug down-up whatever pools
in glasses, cups.
They pile in every forbidden treat.
By day's end, they're spinning like tops,
and their bodies have to be leveled
like Sault Ste.-Marie locks.

I, their mentor, spiel of perseverance,
give the coach-prompts, cheerlead,
cajole them into thinking of what they'll want
to see at 40, knowing all the while
they're child-myopic, primed for barrier break,
focused and insistent on right this minute.

Why bother one more try?
I take a breath and tell myself, before I talk to them,
that life is an unfolding artichoke or blooming onion,
a globe of layers and taste and leaves.
To know it, you must coax yourself
to savor, to peel, to feel.
You must want to touch it with
your perforated finger tips.

You must be glad enough to bump it once again
against your bruise marks.
You must trust that it is good at heart.
That it wants your zest and effort.
That it will, if you can stay the course,
keep opening up.

Today, again, as I have since before their parents were born,
I do my work, my play, my diet, my tests, my shots.

After

After a sick dog night,
slow sips, steady chews of grass,
sniffs of fresh pinestraw.

Another 3 A.M.

Once, at prime time for the plunge to zero in the brain cells;
once, at prime time for the kick-box swell of instinct for survival;
once I woke to what must be nearly the worst of it:
groping knee-jerk, saturated sheets, a V of dark before eyes
that wouldn't, wouldn't focus,
legs that oozed down to the musty carpet floor
instead of making two, three steps to orange juice and candy nip.

My breath, so says a curdled memory, came short.
Then began the groans as I crawled, struggled to half-kneel,
spilled, heaved, swung, crumpled into guitar, chair,
marble edge of antique fireplace, dresser that popped drawers.
The door, instead of opening when I gave a rag doll press,
slammed shut. Vise-like.
Bricking me in like Poe's pathetic Montresor
come to see Fortunato's priceless amontillado.

All there was to do was face the rug's fuzz
and squinch my eyes to see, as always happens
when sugar bottoms near 25 or 30,
the Rorschach black squiggling wider into white.

I moaned for help.
To God. To anyone.
To any sonar-driven bat
skimming near my blanked-out windows.

There was a bathroom-goer's voice, then quick runs up
the mansion's ancient, snapping stairs,
grape juice in a toothpaste glass.

Next, my voice, ear-muffed and seeming rooms away,
wondering if I had had a stroke,
asking in a 5-year-old's vocabulary.

EMT's came, fire-flashing on the road below,
lights oranging up the three flights inside.
Then a passel of them, climbing loud with gear,
hoisting me, bouncing my dead weight down all those stairs.

Jellied hours later, I'm sent home.
They left me off to rest in that same room,
unthinking of the vulture grins that would surely
ceiling down on me.

I dozed, finally, into a retrospect of country home and wooden table,
a winter flick of icy twigs on a second-storey window,
deer outside the lunch nook gnawing late fall apples.
Then an alley of row houses out in Queens
and a scrabble of cowboys, games of statues, tag, hot hopscotch,
trikes, bikes, skate keys.
Lily of the valley in a two-foot front yard,
a grape arbor in the clothes-lined back,
figs on the Fernandi family's single tree.
Then scullers on the Schuylkill and the skywatch of William Penn.
Rocky's sprint-steps to the art museum.
North of Detroit. New York. Philadelphia.
Then Midway Airport, Chicago,
with its way-back, dive-bomb landing strip.
I rolled somehow across the Mackinac,
flickered by train and bridge lights past Pittsburgh,
scanned October foliage through the Poconos, the Appalachians, the Alleghenies.
And then forgot.

Somehow the ER had tubed a travelogue into, then out, of me.
The gurney had dragged a bundle of anxious cargo,
then jettisoned it—which is to say, me—back to that one room's bed,
away from everywhere I'd lived and everyone I'd left.

I waited for a phone to ring, a bell, for someone to talk, to ask,
to say something sad and sympathetic and sassy and smart
to my bashes and cuts.
I waited for something not the least bit befuddled,
something honey-sweet and altogether unnecessary.
I waited for someone to remember my memories.
Or maybe pray over, instead of for, me.

Long, long afterwards I lit one light.
All night.
Each night.
As if a bulb could finally save me.

Now, in a world of new space, new state, new housemates
in arms' reach,
I've begun to forget the night I forgot the splotches of where and how.
Today I can replay these fractions of it.

Sometimes I even sidle into confident, unshocking sleep.

Making Tracks

The heart-hooves of deer,
the wet paw prints of house pet after rain,
the stretch marks of the loggerheads
and scratch of every water bird prancing on damp sand.
Behind, and underneath, a soundtrack
of cheeps and caws and tweets and trills
and mews and grunts and honks and barks.

On my finger pads the blackheads of scabs from finger sticks.
On my upper arms, my legs, my abdomen
the manic tattoo splats of black, violet, maroon, blue,
and grungy old yellow needle marks.

Good morning, I smile, to the gracious and grumps.

All of us do what we can—with noise, with clomp,
with grab for grub, with step indent, with sniff—
to tell the world we're here and think
(they call it chutzpah) that we deserve to be.

PTSD

Had there not been Gulf wars with shaken returnees, I would not have known a name for it. Events can quake our insides, addle our nerve ends, snap our synapses and send them screwy. We can look back years later and see that the aftermaths of trauma and erroneous medication changed our handwriting as well as our wiring.

For months and months every siren at night, every threat of loss, every unthinking word can drive a person into a desert where, like Elijah of old, it seems that a closing of eyes and a shut-down of awareness are the only inviting things. Even an offer of water and hearth cake seem like an attack.

Somewhere along the way, angels may come in. I've had mine in the form of African American men who live on streets or drive white trucks.

When we learn to smile at God-winks or just plain everyday jokes, when we can mock gently or goof around the slightest bit, or jiggle a baby, hope stirs. And once again we feel there may be something to say or think or trust.

Diabetes Makes a Confession

I delight in giving your brain a buzz-cut
when I'm running low on stuff folks
spoon into coffee or sprinkle on cereal,
stuff God and Mother Nature both,
in fiendish back-slap, juice into cherries and corn
and canefields and apple crisp.

I relish soaking you in perspiration till you
almost come to and try to stumble, grope,
what-have-you, for anything sweet.

I've had them squeeze through the pancreas
and decipher insulin just so you and your kind
could live and sometimes whoops into an overdo or overdose.

Control?
You've always liked a degree of it—
a little bit of plan, the slightest smidge of pattern,
but only enough that you, decisive you,
could mess with it and make something new.

It gives me such a kick messing with you.

Number

Oh, you have sugar?

And I'm thinking maybe you mean
the novel by our former student
who moved back to Brooklyn
and then fell into a pool of words
and characters who got mugged and worse.

Uh-uh.

Then I'm thinking maybe you want something instead—
those sweeteners that, one after another,
are guaranteed to make me diarrheic
and off to worship, as one besotted jester put it,
the porcelain goddess scarved in Charmin.

Uh-uh.

So now I'm thinking you're one of those
who oversimplifies, like every hick town noodlehead,
diagnostics. I am not sweet.
More like weary, vulnerable, way more wary of downs than ups,
clutching every moment of normality tight as extenders and
dreadlocks.

Just say IDDM, 250.01, without the slang or coating.

One Blue Heron

Some days are a tired poem,
a crinkled paper,
a crumpled cup,
a discarded plastic bag of dog poop.
All I need is one blue heron.

Then the refuse sinks beneath the mulch.
Something ripples in the water, and something burbles up.
I spy, in high pines, a fledgling nest, a tangle of scraps.
And so remember blood and beat.
I smile upon my pulse and eye beyond the sky.

Three Cars

It had, and has about it still, the swirl
of cinema's rendition of drugged maelstrom,
a wild-with-thirst mirage, a downdraft from
a beaten head, or fever-fueled delirium.

I stopped for gas.
I couldn't find the pump.
I stormed around the car.
I couldn't find the tank.
I got back in.
Drove off.

I couldn't find the lane,
zagged across Route 17,
twirled around an empty parking lot,
slung through a subdivision,
braked at another Phillips 66,
and revisited the routine.
I couldn't find anything.

So I juggernauted north when south was home,
nearly ferried the intracoastal,
lightly vaulted the bridge,
rubbered its sides,
followed the off ramp arrow and the island sign.
Then, crustacean inmate of a crushing haze,
I distinguished a gray and rippling wave of trucks,
traffic turned to roadblock or slammed-shut locks,
a range of traffic lights—what color?—
and three white cars.
Hit.

Hours later I learned the other driver's injuries
would be chiropractic and not lifelong.
Despite a trifle air bag burn,
despite my having kicked with shoeless feet to crack the bashed-in door
just to gulp bare air,
despite the adrenalin that, in a quarter hour, cleared my sight
enough to discover a clump of sand and beach grass where I sat,
despite my mewling, slurring wordlessness,
despite all that,
I seemed, at the ER, oriented to time and place
and substantially unhurt.

An errant hypoglycemic attack, they inferred,
amid a tension of traffic and news.
They'd seen this sort of thing before, they nodded,
as they etched in cuneiform my discharge orders.
The police neither revoked my sobriety nor suspended my license
until such time as someone found a cure.

Insurance settled.
The woman spent her weeks thumped and rolled on a rubber table
and got a timely new Mercedes.

Except for the ambulance lights that for several years kaleidoscoped back,
except for the first time I clenched my teeth and tested twice before taking the wheel,
except for the nights I simmered into wakefulness
when the wind rose and the dog snorted close,
it was case closed.

I've almost forgotten the hurricane watch
that hustled me in the first place
for the octane and nozzle I'd never see.

Sometimes, though, when I begin to drip insistently as rip-tide,
I still cringe at names:
Savannah Highway, Ashley River, Harborview,
James Island, and, of all things,
Folly Beach.
Off the pier there, you see sequins on the Atlantic
and kamikaze kingfishers to this day.

Forgetting Pain

Fix your mind on how to put a truth in word,
a world in verse.

Think of how the revelation of a lifetime
wants a rhythmic line.

Muse on how a universe you'd like to ford
insists it must rehearse

eternal verities in every language, and your rhyme
bridges out a syllable and then calls time.

Remember everything you ever wished
that won't boomerang back.

Make a clumsy poem with no clue,
no code, no crack

at how it is you might say one clear thing
or sound one sure, harmonic ring.

Come back to what is, what was, to what persists
and give in to buzz, to late medicinal fizz.

Until again you lift an idea or a pen.
Until again.

Prescription

Make it easy on yourself:
3 C's.
And thereby scintillate with a new mnemonic.

The first, *Cooperate*,
as in go along with the ebbs and flows,
the carb counts and weigh-ins,
the whatevers in medical breakthroughs and news.

The second, *Combat*,
meaning fight for your life.
Plug holes in the rowboat,
defy the sirens that would woo you to self-pity
and smack your aspirations against a razor-rock cove
and maroon you in a fen of rats and rattle snakes.
Train your internal slugger to pummel all that back.

The third, *Contemplate*
any and all enlargements of the world
and delights as small as the wide fling of cormorant wings
and the skittle of lizard around a front door,
the traces of night chant rising and hushing
from stands of live oak and crape myrtle,
and magnolia blooms bubbling open high as the skylight.

And maybe a fourth: *Come back.*

The Pier at Folly Beach

The dolphins are not dancing today,
but the surfers sit and paddle as if
a too-tall wave may wend in any day,
and the stolid fishers ply their fishing poles
like urgent, hard-wired pick-up sticks
and set their pails in straight, attendant lanes
and fix another day's grizzled gaze,
while on the porches of the oceanfronts
small families pose, teeth gleaming,
into the horizon line where shrimpers skim.

My new doctor, the diabetes specialist, says again
that, over all, I'm well, hearty, nerve-alert, mostly controlled
for one so long a diabetic.
Yet, she warns, those stealth attacks, those chilling dips
into the biochemically induced netherworld,
that space which other aging Boomers might well call a trip,
may come more often
and may be tougher to be dredged up from.
Better, she chirrups, review everything, dawn to dusk, dusk to dawn.
Test, shoot, eat, test, work a little less, test and shoot again, enjoy, rest.
Best do now what's wanting to be done.

The noon sea is grey-green, Atlantic,
and no one here heeds a twit the gale warnings.
The brown thrashers flit to balconies, then bother themselves away
from our outdoor lunch nooks.
I spoon my she-crab soup, sherry-laced and peppery,
nibble salad wafers and a mound of bleu-cheesed greens.
I lemon water down my thoughts—
roughening seas and more incalculable years on insulin.

Out beyond the pier, a solo pelican loops and circles for a quarter hour,
then plunges once, headlong,
for just what it has needed all along.

The Stories

Telling a story does not always let the hearer read the teller's mind. And telling the sensory details and the emotional after-effects does not necessarily reveal the underlying meaning or motive or the end.

Some diabetic episodes are best unraveled by remembering and recounting. It's what helps this protagonist face facts.

Recollection is part of the process of collection. People speak of collecting themselves in the sense of pulling themselves together, coming to the point of being able to encounter the world of others and obligations again.

Recollection in the monastic and liturgical sense is, first of all, quieting. Second, it is summoning into prayer what we know to be true before the One we need. We name certain prayers of summons and summary "collects."

Thus, the pen and key strokes here are not to spin tales of unrelief or grief. They are a massive thank-you that help came, that help comes, and that I fully expect that in future (but transitory) catastrophes whatever help is fitting will come, one way or another. My narratives celebrate the fact that, after a number of near misses, I remain here to swing and sway in a sliver of a universe much larger than my infinitesimal self and much more stuffed with grace than I may, at times, have guessed.

To David Sedaris
(*about his book* Let's Explore Diabetes with Owls)

As if there were a growing multiplex
of the hemoglobin A1C niche market
clamoring for essays.

Molecules of glucose do, for certain, stick to iron,
and that makes for tidy measuring sticks
that endocrinologists can diddle.
But what do fluff and wide eyes
and a taste for night mice barbecued in Africa
have to do with what I
give a hoot to pawn or bargain for or buy?

You lament your age-old receipt of
left-handed compliments and familial put-downs
doled out as rollingly as not quite cubed Jell-o.
A sorry history, a chronic tendency.

But nary a word about my topic.

What was it you wanted from me, your recent readership?
Assurance that you should be a Nobelist
able to speechify as classically and full of mustache as Faulkner?
You're a creative nonfictionist, which means you sometimes lie
or, let's say, stretch.

So, let's deliver this:
The "lol" moments I got reading you galloped incrementally,
and I noticed nicely your #1 status on the NYT book list.
But I'd like to mention that I'd prefer my money back
for your title-only mention of my favorite illness.
That, despite the 30% off, my B&N discount, the coupon.

I want to be your big sister and keep doing this.

More Than a Curriculum Vitae
(for Justice Sotomayor, Type 1 since Age 7)

Overachievers Anonymous.

There are many others to credit,
and even more to emulate,
beyond the rule and realm of empirical evidence,
language, time, prognosis, outer space.

Feet and hearts and kidneys need not always fail,
and certainly not nerve.
Those UFO's that followed you—
those infinite worst case scenarios—
gave way to drones that hovered here and there,
mind-gamed yet unmanned.
And they were expeditiously tamed.

You've check-marked how to woman up.

Diabetes Applauds Itself
(for Brother John Forbis and Mariénne Kreitlow)

I don't like to brag, but I've bestowed some wows of blessings on her. I've focused her life and fueled her for jet propulsion as a pre-emptive strike against a possible early death. Here's the twist. She woke up one morning about two decades back and realized she'd missed her chance to die young. But she still has outbursts of intensity, since no one knows what tomorrow brings.

I've caused her to pay attention to small things. Each day she can turn over dirt and find dozens of wonders, even if they come in the form of earthworms, fire ants, and slugs. Ever since they told her that diabetics often go blind, she's reveled in color and design. She's even cultivated a visual appreciation of German chocolate cakes and peppermint sundaes and found one can admire them like museum art or objects in curio shops without aching with desire to eat them.

She's realized one can theologize but must, in the end, uncomplicate God. Life's too brief to spend it missing the way deity spills out in the swell of Minnesota hills and lakes, geese honk, thunder roll, and new friends with giraffes on their shirts, beads above blouses, and pens in their hands.

Getting Started

I've smoothed the sheets, pulled up the quilt and fluffed
the frosting of pillows, done a soft sweep
of dog hair, socks she's scattered, and the muss
of Milkbone bites she's hid, set out her meat
for breakfast, filled the water bowl, and I have
sauntered down the sidewalk, out to fetch the paper,
yummed back in for berries in my yogurt, noted
the milk and orange juice supply, flavored
coffee with a splash of French vanilla,
and savored the aroma of cloud pink, high pine,
sweetgrass, red mulch, rosebush, pear tree spillover
all before door close and hot dawnlight.

To clarify, I'm in the South and have shot
my Lantus and Humalog, popped
Celebrex, Amlodipine, vitamins, fish oil, and chased the fog.
I know my social media aficionados relish such detail and more.

Meanwhile, this morning's reading from Sirach 30:17
ticked me with a verse about eternal sleep
being better than waggling along chronically sick.
I'm mulling over my online rebuttal along these lines:

Better to be vibrant as possible,
engaged, up and about, ready for work,
cataloguing every simple pleasure and
lauding the day with whatever it takes—
living with some limits, yet defiantly well.

Adventure

It must have been infused in me by a mix of genes and youthful experiences, but, no matter what, I have always felt that there are so many fascinating things to do and there is so much to discover that there is no time to waste lying around waiting for the next meal or the next thing to happen. It makes much more sense to take a role in devising the recipe, crafting the menu, and staging the dinner for the gathering. This approach to life got reinforced, of course, by the convent sages who admonished that it's better to wear out than rust out.

There is also an awful lot to laugh about, even when things don't quite come off as planned. There will surely be a typo in here somewhere.

Pamela Smith's *How Jonathan Green Painted My Momma* was published by Finishing Line Press in 2013. In addition to this chapbook, she has published eleven other books—two collections of poetry, one text on environmental ethics, and eight collections of Biblical meditations. In 2015 she was recipient of a Lilly grant to participate in a convening on "Poetry, Prose, and Prayer" at the Institute for Ecumenical and Cultural Research in Collegeville, Minnesota, and in 2016 and 2017 was awarded a stint as Writer in Residence at the Weymouth Center for the Arts in Southern Pines, North Carolina. She is under contract with Twenty-Third Publications and ACTA Publications for books on the Christian understanding of the Holy Spirit (*Holy Wind, Holy Fire*) and on processing grief (*Acquainted with the Night*) which are slated for release in 2017 and 2018 respectively.

Born in New York City, Pamela Smith has been writing and publishing since the late 1960s. In 1969 she was diagnosed as a Type 1 diabetic. This chapbook contains poems and prose poems relating the grit and gratitude required for living with the demands of this disease.

At present, she is Secretary for Education and Faith Formation for the Catholic Diocese of Charleston in South Carolina. A frequent presenter at retreats and conferences, she also writes a bi-weekly column for a statewide newspaper. She has been a member of the Sisters of Saints Cyril and Methodius since 1972 and has served in a positions ranging from pot washer to general superior.

www.ingramcontent.com/pod-product-compliance
Lightning Source LLC
LaVergne TN
LVHW041517070426
835507LV00012B/1627